THE 30-MINUTE SHAKESPEARE
AS YOU LIKE IT

"Nick Newlin's work as a teaching artist for Folger Education during the past thirteen years has provided students, regardless of their experience with Shakespeare or being on stage, a unique opportunity to tread the boards at the Folger Theatre. Working with students to edit Shakespeare's plays for performance at the annual Folger Shakespeare Festivals has enabled students to gain new insights into the Bard's plays, build their skills of comprehension and critical reading, and just plain have fun working collaboratively with their peers.

Folger Education promotes performance-based teaching of Shakespeare's plays, providing students with an interactive approach to Shakespeare's plays in which they participate in a close reading of the text through intellectual, physical, and vocal engagement. Newlin's *The 30-Minute Shakespeare* series is an invaluable resource for teachers of Shakespeare, and for all who are interested in performing the plays."

ROBERT YOUNG, PH.D.
DIRECTOR OF EDUCATION
FOLGER SHAKESPEARE LIBRARY

As You Like It: The 30-Minute Shakespeare
ISBN 978-1-935550-06-8
Adaptation, essays, and notes ©2018 by Nick Newlin

Cover design by Sarah Juckniess
Printed in the United States of America

Distributed by Consortium Book Sales & Distribution
www.cbsd.com

NICOLO WHIMSEY PRESS
www.30MinuteShakespeare.com

Art Director: Sarah Juckniess
Managing Editors: Katherine Little, Leah Gordon

AS YOU LIKE IT

THE 30-MINUTE SHAKESPEARE

Written by WILLIAM SHAKESPEARE

Abridged AND Edited
by NICK NEWLIN

Nicolo Whimsey
Press

Brandywine, MD

To my sister
Eliza Newlin Carney
for her laughter

Special thanks to Joanne Flynn, Bill Newlin, Eliza Newlin Carney, William and Louisa Newlin, Michael Tolaydo, Hilary Kacser, Sarah Juckniess, Katherine Little, Eva Zimmerman, Leah Gordon, Julie Schaper and all of Consortium, Leo Bowman and the students, faculty, and staff at Banneker Academic High School, and Robert Young Ph.D., and the Folger Shakespeare Library, especially the wonderful Education Department.

✳ TABLE OF CONTENTS

✳ NO EXPERIENCE NECESSARY

I was not a big "actor type" in high school, so if you weren't either, or if the young people you work with are not, then this book is for you. Whether or not you work with "actor types," you can use this book to stage a lively and captivating thirty-minute version of a Shakespeare play. No experience is necessary.

When I was about eleven years old, my parents took me to see Shakespeare's *Two Gentlemen of Verona*, which was being performed as a Broadway musical. I didn't comprehend every word I heard, but I was enthralled with the language, the characters, and the story, and I understood enough of it to follow along. From then on, I associated Shakespeare with *fun*.

Of course Shakespeare is fun. The Elizabethan audiences knew it, which is one reason he was so popular. It didn't matter that some of the language eluded them. The characters were passionate and vibrant, and their conflicts were compelling. Young people study Shakespeare in high school, but more often than not they read his work like a text book and then get quizzed on academic elements of the play, such as plot, theme, and vocabulary. These are all very interesting, but not nearly as interesting as standing up and performing a scene! It is through performance that the play comes alive and all its "academic" elements are revealed. There is nothing more satisfying to a student or teacher than the feeling of "owning" a Shakespeare play, and that can only come from performing it.

But Shakespeare's plays are often two or more hours long, making the performance of an entire play almost out of the question. One can perform a single scene, which is certainly a good start, but what about the story? What about the changes a character goes through as the play progresses? When school groups perform one scene unedited, or when they lump several plays together, the audience can get lost. This is why I have always preferred to tell the story of the play.

The 30-Minute Shakespeare gives students and teachers a chance to get up on their feet and act out a Shakespeare play in half an hour, using his language. The emphasis is on key scenes, with narrative bridges between scenes to keep the audience caught up on the action. The stage directions are built into this script so that young actors do not have to stand in one place; they can move and tell the story with their actions as well as their words. And it can all be done in a classroom during class time!

That is where this book was born: not in a research library, a graduate school lecture, a professional stage, or even an after-school drama club. All of the play cuttings in *The 30-Minute Shakespeare* were first rehearsed in a D.C. public high school English class, and performed successfully at the Folger Shakespeare Library's annual Secondary School Shakespeare Festival. The players were not necessarily "actor types." For many of them, this was their first performance in a play.

Something almost miraculous happens when students perform Shakespeare. They "get" it. By occupying the characters and speaking the words out loud, students gain a level of understanding and appreciation that is unachievable by simply reading the text. That is the magic of a performance-based method of learning Shakespeare, and this book makes the formerly daunting task of staging a Shakespeare play possible for anybody.

With *The 30-Minute Shakespeare* book series I hope to help teachers and students produce a Shakespeare play in a short amount of time, thus jump-starting the process of discovering the beauty, magic, and fun of the Bard. Plot, theme, and language reveal themselves through the performance of these half-hour play cuttings, and everybody involved receives the priceless gift of "owning" a piece of Shakespeare. The result is an experience that is fun and engaging, and one that we can all carry with us as we play out our own lives on the stages of the world.

NICK NEWLIN
Brandywine, MD
March 2010

CHARACTERS IN THE PLAY

The following is a list of characters that appear in this cutting of As You Like It.

Twenty-three actors performed in the original production. This number can be increased to about thirty or decreased to about twelve by having actors share or double roles.

For the full breakdown of characters, see Sample Program.

DUKE SENIOR: Living in banishment

DUKE FREDERICK: Duke Senior's brother, and usurper of his dominions

ROSALIND: Daughter to the banished Duke Senior

CELIA: Rosalind's cousin, daughter to Duke Frederick

AMIENS
JAQUES } Lords attending on the banished Duke

OLIVER
ORLANDO } Sons of Sir Rowland de Boys

TOUCHSTONE: A clown

CORIN: A shepherd

SILVIUS: A young shepherd in love

AUDREY: A goat keeper

PHEBE: A shepherdess

HYMEN: Goddess of Marriage

ADDITIONAL LORDS IN FOREST

SHEEP and **GOATS**

NARRATORS

✳ **SCENE 1.** (ACT I, SCENE III)

A room in Duke Frederick's palace.

STAGEHANDS *place a table, set with teacups and a vase with flowers, and two chairs downstage center.*

Enter **NARRATOR** *from stage rear, coming downstage left.*

As **NARRATOR** *introduces the* **DUKES**, *they enter from designated sides of the stage, cross in character, and exit the opposite side of the stage (see Performance Notes).*

> Our play begins in the court of the hateful Duke Frederick, who has banished his brother, the former Duke Senior, to the forest of Arden, and now banishes his niece Rosalind as well. Rosalind and her cousin, Duke Frederick's daughter Celia, devise a plan to escape to the forest together.

Exit **NARRATOR** *stage left.*

SOUND OPERATOR *plays* Sound Cue #1 ("Palace music").

Enter **CELIA** *and* **ROSALIND** *from stage rear.* **ROSALIND** *sits stage left of the table and* **CELIA** *sits stage right.*

CELIA

> Why, cousin Rosalind! Is it possible, on such a sudden, you should fall into so strong a liking with old Sir Rowland's youngest son?

ROSALIND

The duke my father loved his father dearly.

CELIA

Doth it therefore ensue that you should love his son dearly?

ROSALIND

Let me love him for that, and do you love him because I do. Look, here comes the duke.

CELIA

With his eyes full of anger.

Enter DUKE FREDERICK *from stage right.*

DUKE FREDERICK

Mistress, dispatch you with your safest haste
And get you from our court.

ROSALIND

Me, uncle?

DUKE FREDERICK

You, cousin
Within these ten days if that thou be'st found
So near our public court as twenty miles,
Thou diest for it.

ROSALIND *(falls to her knees)*
I do beseech your grace,
Let me the knowledge of my fault bear with me.

DUKE FREDERICK

Thou art thy father's daughter; there's enough.
(turns his back to her, walks a few paces stage right, and stops with arms crossed)

CELIA *(rushes to* **ROSALIND'S** *side; puts a hand on her shoulder to comfort her)*
If she be a traitor, why so am I.
Pronounce that sentence then on me, my liege:
I cannot live out of her company.

DUKE FREDERICK *(to* **CELIA***)*
You are a fool. *(to* **ROSALIND***)* You, niece, if you
outstay the time, upon mine honor,
And in the greatness of my word, you die.

ROSALIND *buries her face in her hands.*

Exit **DUKE FREDERICK** *stage right.*

CELIA *(kneeling by* **ROSALIND'S** *side)*
O my poor Rosalind, whither wilt thou go?
Wilt thou change fathers? I will give thee mine.
Let my father seek another heir.
Therefore devise with me how we may fly,
I'll go along with thee.

ROSALIND
Why, whither shall we go?

CELIA *(stands, looking stage left)*
To seek my uncle in the forest of Arden.

ROSALIND *(goes to* **CELIA'S** *side, looking stage left)*
Alas, what danger will it be to us,
Maids as we are, to travel forth so far!
Beauty provoketh thieves sooner than gold.
Were it not better,
That I did suit me all points like a man?

ROSALIND *walks downstage, taking on a mannish stride and voice. She grabs a candle and starts to wave it about like a sword, leaping up onto a chair. All of this delights* CELIA *greatly.*

> We'll have a swashing and a martial outside,
> As many other mannish cowards have
> That do outface it with their semblances.

CELIA *(crosses to the chair* ROSALIND *is standing on, curtsies,*
and bats her eyes flirtatiously)
> What shall I call thee when thou art a man?

ROSALIND *(walks to the front of the table, still swaggering)*
> I'll have no worse a name than Jove's own page;
> And therefore look you call me Ganymede.
> *(stops, looks back at* CELIA, *then forward again)*
> But what will you be call'd?

CELIA *(comes downstage, facing out)*
> Something that hath a reference to my state
> No longer Celia, but Aliena. *(brings her hand across*
> *her face mysteriously as if revealing the*
> *character)*

ROSALIND *(has an idea; turns to* CELIA, *excited and happy)*
> But, cousin, what if we assay'd to steal
> The clownish fool out of your father's court?
> Would he not be a comfort to our travel?

CELIA *(agrees enthusiastically)*
> He'll go along o'er the wide world with me.
> *(mischievously)* Leave me alone to woo him.
> Let's away.

Exit CELIA *and* ROSALIND *stage right.*

STAGEHANDS *remove table and chairs, set short stool (tree stump) downstage center and slightly right and tall stool (short tree) downstage left, and scatter a few leaves.*

✳ SCENE 2. (ACT II, SCENE I)

The Forest of Arden.

SOUND OPERATOR *plays* Sound Cue #2 ("Forest music").

Enter **NARRATOR** *from stage rear, coming downstage left.*

As **NARRATOR** *introduces the roles, players enter from designated sides of the stage, cross in character, and exit the opposite side of the stage (see Performance Notes).*

> In the Forest of Arden, Duke Senior and his exiled lords make the best of their life in the woods, where they meet Orlando, who himself has been cast out by his older brother Oliver.

Exit **NARRATOR** *stage left.*

SOUND OPERATOR *plays* Sound Cue #3 ("Forest music").

Enter **DUKE SENIOR**, **AMIENS**, *and one or two extra* **LORDS**, *like foresters, singing "Blow Wind Blow."*

DUKE SENIOR *(stands center, flanked by* **AMIENS** *on his right and another lord on his left, pats them both on the shoulders)*
Now, my co-mates and brothers in exile,
Are not these woods
More free from peril than the envious court?
Sweet are the uses of adversity,
Which finds tongues in trees *(gestures upward),*

books in the running brooks *(gestures downward)*,
Sermons in stones *(picks up a rock and pretends to
   listen to it)* and good in every thing. *(passes
   stone to* AMIENS, *who looks at it, puts it to his
   ear, and shrugs)*
I would not change it.

AMIENS *(admiringly)*
  Happy is your grace,
  That can translate the stubbornness of fortune
  Into so quiet and so sweet a style.

They sit down to eat, pulling out fruit and bread from their packs.

Enter JAQUES *from stage left.*

DUKE SENIOR
  Why, how now, Monsieur Jaques! *(surprised at
    JAQUES'S happy demeanor)*
  What, you look merrily!

JAQUES
  A fool, a fool! I met a fool i' the forest,
  A motley fool; *(begins to prance about merrily, then
    stops sadly)* a miserable world!
  (drops to his knees)
  O that I were a fool!
  (kneels and faces AMIENS, *desperate to make his point)*
  I must have liberty as the wind,
  To blow on whom I please;
  for so fools have; *(blows on* AMIENS, *who holds his
    nose and recoils)*
  But who comes here? *(stands and backs up a few
    paces to observe)*

Enter ORLANDO *from stage left, in a slight panic, sword drawn.*

ORLANDO
> Forbear, and eat no more.

JAQUES *(noticing that the others have food and he doesn't)*
> Why, I have eat none yet.

DUKE SENIOR *(polite but cautious)*
> What would you have?

ORLANDO *(still threatening)*
> I almost die for food; and let me have it.

DUKE SENIOR *(graciously gesturing)*
> Sit down and feed, and welcome to our table.

ORLANDO
> Speak you so gently? *(humbly on one knee, bows)*
> Pardon me, I pray you:
> I thought that all things had been savage here;
> *(sincerely and sadly)* If ever you have look'd on
>   better days,
> If ever from your eyelids wiped a tear
> Let gentleness my strong enforcement be:
> In the which hope I blush, and hide my sword.
>   *(puts his sword back in sheath)*

DUKE SENIOR
> True is it that we have seen better days.

ORLANDO
> Then but forbear your food a little while,
> Whiles, like a doe, I go to find my fawn.

Exit **ORLANDO** *stage right.*

DUKE SENIOR *(to* JAQUES*)*
> Thou seest we are not all alone unhappy:
> This wide and universal theatre
> Presents more woeful pageants than the scene
> Wherein we play in.

JAQUES *(pauses)*
> All the world's a stage,
> And all the men and women merely players:
> *(walks stage right)*
> They have their exits and their entrances;
> And one man in his time plays many parts,
> Last scene of all,
> That ends this strange eventful history,
> Is second childishness and mere oblivion,
> Sans teeth, sans eyes, sans taste, sans everything.
> > *(long pause while the men absorb this image)*

DUKE SENIOR *(realizing the mood has dropped, to* AMIENS*)*
> Give us some music; and, good cousin, sing.

ALL *(sung as they exit)*
> Blow, blow, thou winter wind.
> Thou art not so unkind
> As man's ingratitude;
> Thy tooth is not so keen,
> Because thou art not seen,
> Although thy breath be rude.
> Heigh-ho! Sing, heigh-ho! Unto the green holly:
> Most friendship is feigning, most loving mere folly:
> Then, heigh-ho, the holly!
> This life is most jolly.
> Heigh-ho!

Exit ALL *stage right.*

✳ SCENE 3 (ACT III, SCENE II)

Enter **NARRATOR** *from stage rear, coming downstage left.*

As **NARRATOR** *introduces the roles, players enter from designated sides of the stage, cross in character, and exit the opposite side of the stage (see Performance Notes).*

> Orlando hangs love notes for Rosalind in the forest, while Touchstone the Fool and Corin the Shepherd discuss the merits of court versus country life. Rosalind, as Ganymede, and Celia, as Aliena, discover the love notes and meet the lovestruck Orlando.

Exit **NARRATOR** *stage left.*

Enter **ORLANDO** *from stage right. He hangs a piece of paper on the tree.*

ORLANDO
> Hang there, my verse, in witness of my love:
> O Rosalind! These trees shall be my books
> Run, run, Orlando; carve on every tree
> The fair, the chaste and unexpressive she.

Exit **ORLANDO** *stage rear.*

Enter **CORIN** *and* **TOUCHSTONE** *from stage left. They pause, and* **TOUCHSTONE** *whistles.*

Enter **SHEEP**. **SHEEP** *pass by* **TOUCHSTONE** *and* **CORIN** *and stop to graze downstage right.* **CORIN** *looks at them affectionately and notices one is missing. He whistles again.*

Enter final SHEEP *slowly, looks at audience indignantly. Other* SHEEP *bleat, and the final* SHEEP *joins them.*

CORIN

And how like you this shepherd's life, Master Touchstone?

TOUCHSTONE

Truly, shepherd, in respect it is in the fields, it pleaseth me well; but in respect it is not in the court, it is tedious. Wast ever in court, shepherd?

CORIN

No, truly.

TOUCHSTONE

Then thou art damned.

CORIN

For not being at court? Your reason.

TOUCHSTONE

Why, if thou never wast at court, thou never sawest good manners; if thou never sawest good manners, then thy manners must be wicked; and wickedness is sin, and sin is damnation, shepherd.

CORIN *(tends to one of his sheep)*

Touchstone: those that are good manners at the court are as ridiculous in the country as the behavior of the country is most mockable at the court. You told me you salute not at the court, but you kiss your hands: that courtesy would be uncleanly, if courtiers were shepherds.

TOUCHSTONE

Instance, briefly.

CORIN

Why, we are still handling our ewes, and their fells, you know, are greasy. *(offers his hand for* TOUCHSTONE *to kiss;* TOUCHSTONE *pretends to kiss* CORIN'S *hand but instead kisses his own)*

TOUCHSTONE

Why, do not your courtier's hands sweat? And is not the grease of a mutton as wholesome as the sweat of a man?

CORIN

You have too courtly a wit for me: I'll rest. Here comes young Master Ganymede, my new mistress's brother.

Enter ROSALIND *from stage right with a paper, reading.*

ROSALIND

From the east to western Ind,
No jewel is like Rosalind.
Let no fair be kept in mind
But the fair of Rosalind.

TOUCHSTONE

If a hart do lack a hind,
Let him seek out Rosalind.
Sweetest nut hath sourest rind,
Such a nut is Rosalind.
He that sweetest rose will find
Must find love's prick and Rosalind. *(presents her
            with a rose)*

ROSALIND

Peace, you dull fool! Here comes my sister, reading: stand aside.

Enter CELIA *from stage right, reading.*

CELIA

Nature presently distilled
Helen's cheek, but not her heart,
Cleopatra's majesty,
Atalanta's better part,
Sad Lucretia's modesty.
Rosalind of many parts
Of many faces, eyes and hearts,
Heaven would that she these gifts should have,
And I to live and die her slave.
(to CORIN *and* TOUCHSTONE*)*
How now! Back, friends! Shepherd, go off a little.
Go with him, sirrah.

TOUCHSTONE

Come, shepherd, let us make an honorable retreat.

Exit CORIN *and* TOUCHSTONE *stage right.* CELIA *and* ROSALIND *look at* SHEEP, *which also exit.*

CELIA

Did'st thou hear without wondering how thy name should be hanged and carved upon these trees? Trow you who hath done this? *(holds paper out to* ROSALIND; ROSALIND *reaches for it, and* CELIA *pulls it away)*

ROSALIND

I prithee now tell me who it is.

CELIA

> O wonderful, wonderful, and most wonderful
> wonderful! And yet again wonderful, and after that,
> out of all hooping!

ROSALIND

> I prithee take the cork out of thy mouth, that I may
> drink thy tidings.

CELIA

> So you may put a man in your belly. *(both giggle)*
> It is young Orlando.

ROSALIND

> Orlando?

CELIA

> Orlando.

ROSALIND *(shocked, looking down at her men's clothes)*

> Alas the day! What shall I do with my doublet and
> hose? What did he when thou sawest him? What
> said he? How looked he? Did he ask for me? Where
> remains he? and when shalt thou see him again?
> Answer me in one word.

CELIA *(begins to answer)*

> You must borrow me Gargantua's mouth first—

ROSALIND *(interrupting)*

> But doth he know that I am in this forest and in
> man's apparel? Sweet, say on.

CELIA

> I found him under a tree like a dropped acorn.
> Soft! Comes he not here?

ROSALIND

> 'Tis he: slink by, and note him.

ROSALIND *hides behind stage right pillar and* CELIA *hides behind stage left pillar.*

(Aside to CELIA*)* I will speak to him, like a saucy lackey and
> under that habit play the knave with him.

Enter ORLANDO *from stage left, with papers.*

ROSALIND *swaggers out from behind pillar but keeps her distance from* ORLANDO. *She speaks in a low, mannish tone.*

ROSALIND

> Do you hear, forester?

ORLANDO

> Very well: what would you?

ROSALIND

> There is a man haunts the forest, that abuses our
> young plants with carving "Rosalind" on their barks;
> if I could meet that fancy-monger I would give
> him some good counsel, for he seems to have the
> quotidian of love upon him.

ORLANDO

> I am he that is so love-shaked: I pray you tell me
> your remedy.

ROSALIND *(turns away)*

> Love is merely a madness, *(turns back and takes a few steps toward* **ORLANDO***)* Yet I profess curing it by counsel.

ORLANDO

> Did you ever cure any so?

ROSALIND

> Yes, one, and in this manner. He was to imagine me his love, his mistress; and I set him every day to woo me, and thus I cured him. *(with each word she moves a little closer, until they are nearly touching)*

ORLANDO *(confused at his attraction to her; turns away, flustered)*

> I would not be cured, youth.

ROSALIND *(turns him around and approaches him again)*

> I would cure you, if you would but call me Rosalind and come every day to my cote and woo me. *(holds out her hand)* Will you go?

ORLANDO *(takes her hand)*

> With all my heart, good youth.

ROSALIND

> Nay you must call me Rosalind. Come, sister, will you go?

CELIA *comes out from behind tree giggling.*

Exit **ALL** *stage left.*

✳ **SCENE 4** (ACT III, SCENE III)

Enter NARRATOR *from stage rear, coming downstage left.*

NARRATOR
> Touchstone has a strong attraction to the simple goatherder Audrey, who does not seem to understand his witticisms very well.

Exit NARRATOR *stage right.*

Enter AUDREY *from stage right with a bucket, followed by* GOATS *(including* NARRATOR*). She struggles to keep the unruly* GOATS *in line.*

TOUCHSTONE
> Come apace, good Audrey. I will fetch up your goats, Audrey.

TOUCHSTONE *attempts to catch a* GOAT *but the* GOAT *bleats and tries to eat* TOUCHSTONE'S *costume.* TOUCHSTONE *gives the* GOAT *a handkerchief to eat instead, and then turns toward* AUDREY *and regains his composure. He brushes off a tree stump with his handkerchief and seats* AUDREY *there.*

> And, how now, Audrey. Am I the man yet? Doth my simple feature content you? *(poses to her right)*

AUDREY *(looks him up and down, confusedly)*
> Your features, Lord warrant us!
> *(pause)* What features?

TOUCHSTONE *(tiptoes among the* GOATS, *who are still trying to eat his costume)*
I am here with thee and thy goats, as the most capricious poet, honest Ovid, was among the Goths. *(*AUDREY *looks at him uncomprehending)* Truly, I would the gods had made thee poetical.

AUDREY *(pretends to understand, nods her head, and pauses)*
I do not know what "poetical" is. Is it honest in deed and word? Is it a true thing?

TOUCHSTONE *(kneels, facing* AUDREY*)*
No, truly, for the truest poetry is the most feigning, and lovers are given to poetry. *(tries to kiss her hand, but she turns away)*

AUDREY
Would you not have me honest?

TOUCHSTONE *(moves to the other side of* AUDREY *and kneels again)*
Truly, and to cast away honesty upon a foul slut were to put good meat into an unclean dish. *(tries to kiss her hand again, but she stands up, and* TOUCHSTONE *falls over onto the stump)*

AUDREY *(stands downstage right)*
I am not a slut, although I thank the gods I am foul *(thinks she is flattering herself, not knowing the meaning of the words she speaks)*

TOUCHSTONE
Well, praised be the gods for thy foulness; sluttishness may come hereafter. But be it as it may be, I will marry thee. *(approaches her and kisses her hand)*

AUDREY *(blushing, looks up to the heavens)*
>Well, the gods give us joy.

TOUCHSTONE
>Come, sweet Audrey. We must be married, or we
>must live in bawdry.

Exit **AUDREY** *and* **TOUCHSTONE** *stage right, arm in arm, followed by* **GOATS**.

✳ **SCENE 5** (ACT III, SCENE V)

Another part of the forest.

Enter **NARRATOR** *stage right, still chewing on the handkerchief.*

> Silvius, a lovestruck shepherd, vainly woos
> the scornful Phebe, who falls for Rosalind
> (as Ganymede). Nothing is simple in love!

Exit **NARRATOR** *stage left.*

Enter **PHEBE** *and* **SILVIUS** *from rear curtain.* **PHEBE** *walks to the far end of stage right and stands with arms crossed.*

SILVIUS *runs over and kneels at* **PHEBE'S** *feet, grabbing at her knees. She tries to kick him loose.*

SILVIUS
> Sweet Phebe, do not scorn me;
> If ever you meet in some fresh cheek
> the power of fancy,
> Then shall you know the wounds invisible
> That love's keen arrows make.

Enter **ROSALIND** *from stage left, followed by* **NARRATOR**. *They observe* **PHEBE** *and* **SILVIUS**.

PHEBE *(shakes* **SILVIUS** *loose; looks down at him with contempt)*
> But till that time
> Come not thou near me: and when that time comes,

Afflict me with thy mocks, pity me not;
As till that time I shall not pity thee.

ROSALIND *(moves toward* **PHEBE***)*

And why, I pray you? What though you have no
    beauty,—
Must you be therefore proud and pitiless?

PHEBE *stares at* **ROSALIND**, *lovestruck; she steps over* **SILVIUS**,
barely missing his head.

Why, what means this? Why do you look on me?
(to **CELIA***)* I think she means to tangle my eyes too!
*(***CELIA** *tries to keep from lauging at this idea)*
(as **PHEBE** *approaches,* **ROSALIND** *extends her arm,*
halting **PHEBE'S** *progress)*
No, faith, proud mistress, hope not after it. *(***PHEBE**
    keeps trying)
(to **SILVIUS***)* You foolish shepherd, wherefore do you
    follow her,
Like foggy south puffing with wind and rain?
'tis such fools as you
That makes the world full of ill-favor'd children:
(to **PHEBE***)* Mistress, sell when you can: you are not
    for all markets:
Cry the man mercy; love him; take his offer:
Foul is most foul, being foul to be a scoffer.
So take her to thee, shepherd: fare you well. *(begins*
    to exit stage left, but **PHEBE** *grabs her hand)*

PHEBE

Sweet youth, I pray you, chide a year together: I had
rather hear you chide than this man woo.

ROSALIND *(to* **PHEBE***)*

He's fallen in love with your foulness *(to* **CELIA***)*

and she'll fall in love with my anger. I'll sauce her
with bitter words.
(to PHEBE*)* Why look you so upon me?
I pray you, do not fall in love with me,
For I am falser than vows made in wine:
Besides, I like you not.
(to SILVIUS*)* Shepherd, ply her hard. *(turns* SILVIUS
physically toward Phebe, giving him a little push)

Exit ROSALIND *and* CELIA *stage left.*

PHEBE *(gazes lovestruck after* ROSALIND*)*
"Who ever loved that loved not at first sight?"

SILVIUS *(kneels at* PHEBE'S *feet and hugs her leg)*
Sweet Phebe,—

PHEBE *(shakes him off her leg again)*
Ha, what say'st thou, Silvius?

SILVIUS *(props himself up, musters up his strength and dignity)*
I would have you.

PHEBE *(softens just a bit)*
Silvius, the time was that I hated thee,
But since that thou canst talk of love so well,
Thy company, I will endure. *(helps him up)*

SILVIUS
Loose now and then
A scatter'd smile, and that I'll live upon.

PHEBE *(gives him a quick, fake smile before thinking wistfully
of* ROSALIND *again)*
Know'st now the youth that spoke to me erewhile?

SILVIUS

Not very well, but I have met him oft.

PHEBE

Think not I love him, though I ask for him:
There was a pretty redness in his lip,
The best thing in him is his complexion.
I love him not nor hate him not; *(angering a bit)* and
yet I have more cause to hate him than to love him:
For what had he to do to chide at me?
I will be bitter with him and passing short.
Go with me, Silvius. *(grabs his arm and half-drags
        him offstage right)*

SILVIUS

Phebe, with all my heart!

Exit **PHEBE** *and* **SILVIUS** *stage right.*

✳ **SCENE 6** (ACT V, SCENE II)

The forest.

Enter NARRATOR *from stage rear, coming downstage left.*

> Oliver, having reconciled with his brother Orlando,
> tells of his love for Aliena. Meanwhile, Rosalind
> assures Orlando, Silvius, and Phebe that she can
> solve all of their love woes, and that they will all be
> married the next day.

Exit NARRATOR *stage left.*

Enter ORLANDO *and* OLIVER *from stage curtain, with* ORLANDO *to*
OLIVER'S *left.*

ORLANDO

> Is't possible that on so little acquaintance you should
> like her? That but seeing you should love her? And
> loving woo? And, wooing, she should grant? And
> will you persever to enjoy her?

OLIVER

> Neither call the giddiness of it in question, my
> sudden wooing, nor her sudden consenting;
> I love Aliena; *(drops to his knees)* consent with both
> that we may enjoy each other: it shall be to your
> good; for my father's house and all the revenue that
> was old Sir Rowland's will I estate upon you, and
> here live and die a shepherd. *(bows his head humbly)*

ORLANDO *(looks at the audience, giving them a smile and*
a thumbs up)
You have my consent. Let your wedding be
to-morrow: Go you and prepare Aliena.

Exit **OLIVER** *stage right.*

Enter **ROSALIND** *from stage rear, standing to* **ORLANDO'S** *right.*

ROSALIND
O, my dear Orlando. *(starts to hug him enthusiastically,*
then quickly backs off) Your brother and my sister no
sooner met but they looked, no sooner looked but
they made a pair of stairs to marriage. They are in
the very wrath of love and they will together; clubs
cannot part them.

ORLANDO
They shall be married to-morrow, Ganymede. *(turns*
toward her) But, O, how bitter a thing it is to look
into happiness through another man's eyes!

ROSALIND
Why then, to-morrow I cannot serve your turn for
Rosalind? *(holds his hand, but then relents)*

ORLANDO *(moving away from* **ROSALIND***)*
I can live no longer by thinking.

ROSALIND *(mysteriously)*
Believe then, if you please, that I can do strange
things: I have, since I was three year old, conversed
with a magician. If you do love Rosalind so near the
heart as your gesture cries it out, when your brother
marries Aliena, shall you marry her.

Enter PHEBE *and* SILVIUS *from stage right, with* PHEBE *to the left.*

Look, here comes a lover of mine and a lover of hers.

PHEBE *(to* ROSALIND*)*
Youth, you have done me much ungentleness.

ROSALIND
You are there followed by a faithful shepherd;
Look upon him, love him; he worships you.

PHEBE
Good shepherd, tell this youth what 'tis to love.

SILVIUS
It is to be all made of sighs and tears;
And so am I for Phebe. *(looks left to* PHEBE*)*

PHEBE
And I for Ganymede. *(looks left to* ROSALIND*)*

ORLANDO
And I for Rosalind. *(looks right to* ROSALIND*)*

ROSALIND
And I for no woman. *(looks straight out, then quickly
left to* ORLANDO, *then out)*

SILVIUS
It is to be all made of faith and service;
And so am I for Phebe.

PHEBE
And I for Ganymede.

ORLANDO

> And I for Rosalind.

ROSALIND

> And I for no woman.

SILVIUS

> It is to be all made of fantasy,
> All made of passion and all made of wishes,
> And so am I for Phebe.

PHEBE

> And so am I for Ganymede.

ORLANDO

> And so am I for Rosalind.

ROSALIND

> And so am I for no woman.
> Pray you, no more of this; 'tis like the howling of
> Irish wolves against the moon. *(to* SILVIUS*)* I will
> help you, if I can: *(to* PHEBE*)* I would love you, if I
> could. To-morrow meet me all together. *(to* PHEBE*)*
> I will marry you, if ever I marry woman, and I'll be
> married to-morrow: *(to* ORLANDO, *passionately)* I will
> satisfy you, if ever I satisfied man, and you shall be
> married to-morrow: *(to* SILVIUS*)* I will content you,
> if what pleases you contents you, and you shall be
> married to-morrow.

Exit ALL *stage right.*

✳ SCENE 7. (ACT V, SCENE IV)

The forest.

STAGEHANDS *bring throne downstage center.*

Enter **NARRATOR** *from stage rear, coming downstage left.*

NARRATOR

> The Goddess of Marriage, Hymen, arrives to bring
> the lovers together and the comedy to a merry ending.

Exit **NARRATOR** *stage left.*

SOUND OPERATOR *plays* Sound Cue #4 ("Magical wedding music").

Enter **DUKE SENIOR, ORLANDO, OLIVER, TOUCHSTONE,** *and* **SILVIUS** *from stage rear.*

DUKE SENIOR

> Dost thou believe, Orlando, that the boy
> Can do all this that he hath promised?

ORLANDO

> I sometimes do believe, and sometimes do not;
> As those that fear they hope, and know they fear.

Enter **HYMEN, ROSALIND, CELIA, AUDREY,** *and* **PHEBE** *from stage rear. Each woman stands to the right of her husband-to-be.* **PHEBE** *looks over at* **ROSALIND** *in amazement.*

HYMEN

With great importance and godliness
Then is there mirth in heaven,
When earthly things made even
Atone together.
Good duke, receive thy daughter
Hymen from heaven brought her,
That thou mightst join her hand with his
Whose heart within his bosom is.

ROSALIND *(to* ORLANDO, *who is looking at her in amazement)*
To you I give myself, for I am yours.

DUKE SENIOR

If there be truth in sight, you are my daughter.

ORLANDO *(in disbelief, but ecstatic)*
If there be truth in sight, you are my Rosalind.

PHEBE *(to* ROSALIND*)*
If sight and shape be true,
Why then, my love adieu!

HYMEN

Peace, ho! I bar confusion: *(snaps her fingers, all
freeze)*
'Tis I must make conclusion
Of these most strange events:
Here's eight that must take hands
To join in Hymen's bands,

HYMEN *waves her hands and all the couples hold hands. She
snaps her fingers again, and all continue to hold hands except*
DUKE SENIOR, *who realizes he's holding hands with* OLIVER *and
abruptly pulls his hand away.*

If truth holds true contents.
Whiles a wedlock-hymn we sing,
Feed yourselves with questioning;
That reason wonder may diminish,
How thus we met, and these things finish.

DUKE SENIOR
Proceed, proceed: we will begin these rites,
As we do trust they'll end, in true delights.

All sing and dance, adding in percussion.

ALL
It was a lover and his lass
With a hey, and a ho, and a hey-nonny-no,
That o'er the green cornfield did pass
In springtime, the only pretty ring time,
When birds do sing, hey ding a ding, ding.
Sweet lovers love the spring.
And therefore take the present time,
With a hey, and a ho, and a hey-nonny no,
For love is crowned with the prime,
In springtime, the only pretty ring time,
When birds do sing, hey ding a ding, ding.
Sweet lovers love the spring.

All hold hands and take a bow. Exeunt.

✳ PERFORMING SHAKESPEARE

HOW *THE 30-MINUTE SHAKESPEARE* WAS BORN

In 1981 I performed a "Shakespeare Juggling" piece called "To Juggle or Not To Juggle" at the first Folger Library Secondary School Shakespeare Festival. The audience consisted of about 200 Washington, D.C. area high school students who had just performed thirty-minute versions of Shakespeare plays for each other and were jubilant over the experience. I was dressed in a jester's outfit, and my job was to entertain them. I juggled and jested and played with Shakespeare's words, notably Hamlet's "To be or not to be" soliloquy, to very enthusiastic response. I was struck by how much my "Shakespeare Juggling" resonated with a group who had just performed Shakespeare themselves. "Getting" Shakespeare is a heady feeling, especially for adolescents, and I am continually delighted at how much joy and satisfaction young people derive from performing Shakespeare. Simply reading and studying this great playwright does not even come close to inspiring the kind of enthusiasm that comes from performance.

Surprisingly, many of these students were not "actor types." A good percentage of the students performing Shakespeare that day were part of an English class which had rehearsed the plays during class time. Fifteen years later, when I first started directing plays in D.C. public schools as a Teaching Artist with the Folger Shakespeare Library, I entered a ninth grade English class as a guest and spent two or three days a week for two or three months preparing students for the Folger's annual Secondary School Shakespeare Festival. I have conducted this annual residency with the Folger ever since. Every year for seven action-packed days, eight groups of students between grades seven and twelve tread the boards onstage at the Folger's Elizabethan Theatre, a grand recreation of a sixteenth-century venue with a three-tiered gallery, carved oak columns, and a sky-painted canopy.

As noted on the Folger website (www.folger.edu), "The festival is a celebration of the Bard, not a competition. Festival commentators—drawn from the professional theater and Shakespeare education communities—recognize exceptional performances, student directors, and good spirit amongst the students with selected awards at the end of each day. They are also available to share feedback with the students."

My annual Folger Teaching Artist engagement, directing a Shakespeare play in a public high school English class, is the most challenging and the most rewarding thing I do all year. I hope this book can bring you the same rewards.

GETTING STARTED

GAMES

How can you get an English class (or any other group of young people, or even adults) to start the seemingly daunting task of performing a Shakespeare play? You have already successfully completed the critical first step, which is buying this book. You hold in your hand a performance-ready, thirty-minute cutting of a Shakespeare play, with stage directions to get the actors moving about the stage purposefully. But it's a good idea to warm the group up with some theater games.

One good initial exercise is called "Positive/Negative Salutations." Students stand in two lines facing each other (four or five students in each line) and, reading from index cards, greet each other, first with a "Positive" salutation in Shakespeare's language (using actual phrases from the plays), followed by a "negative" greeting.

Additionally, short vocal exercises are an essential part of the preparation process. The following is a very simple and effective vocal warm-up: Beginning with the number two, have the whole group count to twenty using increments of two (i.e., "Two, four, six . . ."). Increase the volume slightly with each number, reaching top volume with "twenty," and then decrease the volume while counting back down, so that the students are practically whispering when they arrive again at "two." This exercise teaches dynamics and allows them to get loud as a group without any individual pressure. Frequently during a rehearsal period, if a student is mumbling inaudibly, I will refer back to this exercise as a reminder that we can and often do belt it out!

"Stomping Words" is a game that is very helpful at getting a handle on Shakespeare's rhythm. Choose a passage in iambic pentameter and have the group members walk around the room in a circle, stomping their feet on the second beat of each line:

Two **house**-holds, **both** a-**like** in **dig**-nity
In **fair** Ve-**ro**na **Where** we **lay** our **scene**

Do the same thing with a prose passage, and have the students discuss their experience with it, including points at which there is an extra beat, etc., and what, if anything, it might signify.

I end every vocal warm-up with a group reading of one of the speeches from the play, emphasizing diction and projection, bouncing off consonants, and encouraging the group members to listen to each other so that they can speak the lines together in unison. For variety I will throw in some classic "tongue twisters" too, such as, "The sixth sheik's sixth sheep is sick."

The Folger Shakespeare Library's website (http://www.folger.edu) and their book series *Shakespeare Set Free*, edited by Peggy O'Brien, are two great resources for getting started with a performance-based teaching of Shakespeare in the classroom. The Folger website has numerous helpful resources and activities, many submitted by teachers, for helping a class actively participate in the process of getting to know a Shakespeare play. For more simple theater games, Viola Spolin's *Theatre Games for the Classroom* is very helpful, as is one I use frequently, *Theatre Games for Young Performers*.

HATS AND PROPS

Introducing a few hats and props early in the process is a good way to get the action going. Hats, in particular, provide a nice avenue for giving young actors a non-verbal way of getting into character. In the opening weeks, when students are still holding onto their scripts, a hat can give an actor a way to "feel" like a character. Young actors are natural masters at injecting their own personality into what they wear, and even small choices made with how a hat is worn (jauntily, shadily, cockily, mysteriously) provide a starting point for discussion of specific characters, their traits, and their relationships with other characters. All such discussions always lead back to one thing: the text. "Mining the text" is consistently the best strategy for uncovering the mystery of Shakespeare's language. That is where all the answers lie: in the words themselves.

WHAT DO THE WORDS MEAN?

It is essential that young actors know what they are saying when they recite Shakespeare. If not, they might as well be scat singing, riffing on sounds and rhythm but not conveying a specific meaning. The real question is: What do the words mean? The answer is multifaceted, and can be found in more than one place. The New Folger Library paperback editions of the plays themselves (edited by Barbara Mowat and Paul Werstine, Washington Square Press) are a great resource for understanding Shakespeare's words and passages and "translating" them into modern English. These editions also contain chapters on Shakespeare's language, his life, his theater, a "Modern Perspective," and further reading. There is a wealth of scholarship embedded in these wonderful books, and I make it a point to read them cover to cover before embarking on a play-directing project. At the very least, it is a good idea for any adult who intends to direct a Shakespeare play with a group of students to go through the explanatory notes that appear on the pages facing the text. These explanatory notes are an indispensable "translation tool."

The best way to get students to understand what Shakespeare's words mean is to ask them what they think they mean. Students have their own associations with the words and with how they sound and feel. The best ideas on how to perform Shakespeare often come directly from the students, not from anybody else's notion. If a student has an idea or feeling about a word or passage, and it resonates with her emotionally, physically, or spiritually, then Shakespeare's words can be a vehicle for her feelings. That can result in some powerful performances!

I make it my job as director to read the explanatory notes in the Folger text, but I make it clear to the students that almost "anything goes" when trying to understand Shakespeare. There are no wrong interpretations. Students have their own experiences, with some shared and some uniquely their own. If someone has an association with the phrase "canker-blossom," or if the words make that student or his character feel or act a certain way, then that is the "right" way to decipher it.

I encourage the students to refer to the Folger text's explanatory notes and to keep a pocket dictionary handy. Young actors must attach some meaning to every word or line they recite. If I feel an actor is glossing over a word, I will stop him and ask him what he is saying. If he doesn't know, we will figure it out together as a group.

PROCESS VS. PRODUCT

The process of learning Shakespeare by performing one of his plays is more important than whether everybody remembers his lines or whether somebody misses a cue or an entrance. But my Teaching Artist residencies have always had the end goal of a public performance for about 200 other students, so naturally the performance starts to take precedence over the process somewhere around dress rehearsal in the students' minds. It is my job to make sure the actors are prepared—otherwise they will remember the embarrassing moment of a public mistake and not the glorious triumph of owning a Shakespeare play.

In one of my earlier years of play directing, I was sitting in the audience as one of my narrators stood frozen on stage for at least a minute, trying to remember her opening line. I started scrambling in my backpack below my seat for a script, at last prompting her from the audience. Despite her fine performance, that embarrassing moment is all she remembered from the whole experience. Since then I have made sure to assign at least one person to prompt from backstage if necessary. Additionally, I inform the entire cast that if somebody is dying alone out there, it is okay to rescue him or her with an offstage prompt.

There is always a certain amount of stage fright that will accompany a performance, especially a public one for an unfamiliar audience. As a director, I live with stage fright as well, even though I am not appearing on stage. The only antidote to this is work and preparation. If a young actor is struggling with her lines, I make sure to arrange for a session where we run lines over the telephone. I try to set up a buddy system so that students can run lines with their peers, and this often works well. But if somebody does not have a "buddy," I will personally make the time to help out myself. As I assure my students from the outset, I am not going to let them fail or embarrass themselves. They need an experienced leader. And if the leader has experience in teaching but not in directing Shakespeare, then he needs this book!

It is a good idea to culminate in a public performance, as opposed to an in-class project, even if it is only for another classroom. Student actors want to show their newfound Shakespearian thespian skills to an outside group, and this goal motivates them to do a good job. In that respect, "product" is important. Another wonderful bonus to performing a play is that it is a unifying group effort. Students learn teamwork. They learn to give focus to another actor when he is speaking, and to play off of other characters. I like to end each performance with the entire cast reciting a passage in unison. This is a powerful ending, one that reaffirms the unity of the group.

SEEING SHAKESPEARE PERFORMED

It is very helpful for young actors to see Shakespeare performed by a group of professionals, whether they are appearing live on stage (preferable but not always possible) or on film. Because an entire play can take up two or more full class periods, time may be an issue. I am fortunate because thanks to a local foundation that underwrites theater education in the schools, I have been able to take my school groups to a Folger Theatre matinee of the play that they are performing. I always pick a play that is being performed locally that season. But not all group leaders are that lucky. Fortunately, there is the Internet, specifically YouTube. A quick YouTube search for "Shakespeare" can unearth thousands of results, many appropriate for the classroom.

The first "Hamlet" result showed an 18-year-old African-American actor on the streets of Camden, New Jersey, delivering a riveting performance of Hamlet's "The play's the thing." The second clip was from *Cat Head Theatre,* an animation of cats performing Hamlet. Of course, YouTube boasts not just alley cats and feline thespians, but also clips by true legends of the stage, such as John Gielgud and Richard Burton. These clips can be saved and shown in classrooms, providing useful inspiration.

One advantage of the amazing variety of clips available on YouTube is that students can witness the wide range of interpretations for any given scene, speech, or character in Shakespeare, thus freeing them from any preconceived notion that there is a "right" way to do it. Furthermore, modern interpretations of the Bard may appeal to those who are put off by the "thees and thous" of Elizabethan speech.

By seeing Shakespeare performed either live or on film, students are able to hear the cadence, rhythm, vocal dynamics, and pronunciation of the language, and they can appreciate the life that other actors breathe into the characters. They get to see the story told dramatically, which inspires them to tell their own version.

PUTTING IT ALL TOGETHER

THE STEPS

After a few sessions of theater games to warm up the group, it's time to begin the process of casting the play. Each play cutting in *The 30-Minute Shakespeare* series includes a cast list and a sample program, demonstrating which parts have been divided. Cast size is generally between twelve and thirty students, with major roles frequently assigned to more than one performer. In other words, one student may play Juliet in the first scene, another in the second scene, and yet another in the third. This will distribute the parts evenly so that there is no "star of the show." Furthermore, this prevents actors from being burdened with too many lines. If I have an actor who is particularly talented or enthusiastic, I will give her a bigger role. It is important to go with the grain—one cast member's enthusiasm can be contagious.

I provide the performer of each shared role with a similar head-piece and/or cape, so that the audience can keep track of the characters. When there are sets of twins, I try to use blue shirts and red shirts, so that the audience has at least a fighting chance of figuring it out! Other than these costume consistencies, I rely on the text and the audience's observance to sort out the doubling of characters. Generally, the audience can follow because we are telling the story.

Some participants are shy and do not wish to speak at all on stage. To these students I assign non-speaking parts and technical roles such as sound operator and stage manager. However, I always get everybody on stage at some point, even if it is just for the final group speech, because I want every group member to experience what it is like to be on a stage as part of an ensemble.

CASTING THE PLAY

Young people can be self-conscious and nervous with "formal" auditions, especially if they have little or no acting experience.

I conduct what I call an "informal" audition process. I hand out a questionnaire asking students if there is any particular role that they desire, whether they play a musical instrument. To get a feel for them as people, I also ask them to list one or two hobbies or interests. Occasionally this will inform my casting decisions. If someone can juggle, and the play has the part of a Fool, that skill may come in handy. Dancing or martial arts abilities can also be applied to roles.

For the auditions, I do not use the cut script. I have students stand and read from the Folger edition of the complete text in order to hear how they fare with the longer passages. I encourage them to breathe and carry their vocal energy all the way to the end of a long line of text. I also urge them to play with diction, projection, modulation, and dynamics, elements of speech that we have worked on in our vocal warm-ups and theater games.

I base my casting choices largely on reading ability, vocal strength, and enthusiasm for the project. If someone has requested a particular role, I try to honor that request. I explain that even with a small part, an actor can create a vivid character that adds a lot to the play. Wide variations in personality types can be utilized: if there are two students cast as Romeo, one brooding and one effusive, I try to put the more brooding Romeo in an early lovelorn scene, and place the effusive Romeo in the balcony scene. Occasionally one gets lucky, and the doubling of characters provides a way to match personality types with different aspects of a character's personality. But also be aware of the potential serendipity of non-traditional casting. For example, I have had one of the smallest students in the class play a powerful Othello. True power comes from within!

Generally, I have more females than males in a class, so women are more likely (and more willing) to play male characters than vice versa.

Rare is the high school boy who is brave enough to play a female character, which is unfortunate because it can reap hilarious results.

GET OUTSIDE HELP

Every time there is a fight scene in one of the plays I am directing, I call on my friend Michael Tolaydo, a professional actor and theater professor at St. Mary's College, who is an expert in all aspects of theater, including fight choreography. Not only does Michael stage the fight, but he does so in a way that furthers the action of the play, highlighting character's traits and bringing out the best in the student actors. Fight choreography must be done by an expert or somebody could get hurt. In the absence of such help, super slow-motion fights are always a safe bet and can be quite effective, especially when accompanied by a soundtrack on the boom box.

During dress rehearsals I invite my friend Hilary Kacser. a Washington-area actor and dialect coach for two decades. Because I bring her in late in the rehearsal process, I have her direct her comments to me, which I then filter and relay to the cast. This avoids confusing the cast with a second set of directions. This caveat only applies to general directorial comments from outside visitors. Comments on specific artistic disciplines such as dance, music, and stage combat can come from the outside experts themselves.

If you work in a school, you might have helpful resources within your own building, such as a music or dance teacher who could contribute their expertise to a scene. If nobody is available in your school, try seeking out a member of the local professional theater. Many local performing artists will be glad to help, and the students are usually thrilled to have a visit from a professional performer.

LET STUDENTS BRING THEMSELVES INTO THE PLAY

The best ideas often come from the students themselves. If a young actor has a notion of how to play a scene, I will always give that idea a try. In a rehearsal of *Henry IV, Part 1,* one traveler jumped into the other's arms when they were robbed. It got a huge laugh. This was something that they did on instinct. We kept that bit for the performance, and it worked wonderfully.

As a director, you have to foster an environment in which that kind of spontaneity can occur. The students have to feel safe to experiment. In the same production of *Henry IV,* Falstaff and Hal invented a little fist bump "secret handshake" to use in the battle scene. The students were having fun and bringing parts of themselves into the play. Shakespeare himself would have approved. When possible I try to err on the side of fun because if the young actors are having fun, then they will commit themselves to the project. The beauty of the language, the story, the characters, and the pathos will follow.

There is a balance to be achieved here, however. In that same production of *Henry IV, Part 1,* the student who played Bardolph was having a great time with her character. She carried a leather wineskin around and offered it up to the other characters in the tavern. It was a prop with which she developed a comic relationship. At the end of our thirty-minute *Henry IV, Part 1,* I added a scene from *Henry IV, Part 2* as a coda: The new King Henry V (formerly Falstaff's drinking and carousing buddy Hal) rejects Falstaff, banishing him from within ten miles of the King. It is a sad and sobering moment, one of the most powerful in the play.

But at the performance, in the middle of the King's rejection speech (played by a female student, and her only speech), Bardolph offered her flask to King Henry and got a big laugh, thus not only upstaging the King but also undermining the seriousness and poignancy of the whole scene. She did not know any better; she was bringing herself to the character as I had been encouraging her to do. But it was inappropriate, and in subsequent seasons, if I foresaw something like that happening as an individual joyfully occupied a character, I attempted to prevent it. Some things we cannot predict. Now I make sure to issue a statement warning against changing any of the blocking on show day, and to watch out for upstaging one's peers.

FOUR FORMS OF ENGAGEMENT: VOCAL, EMOTIONAL, PHYSICAL, AND INTELLECTUAL

When directing a Shakespeare play with a group of students, I always start with the words themselves because the words have the power to engage the emotions, mind, and body. Also, I start with the words in action, as in the previously mentioned exercise, "Positive and Negative Salutations." Students become physically engaged; their bodies react to the images the words evoke. The words have the power to trigger a switch in both the teller and the listener, eliciting both an emotional and physical reaction. I have never heard a student utter the line "Fie! Fie! You counterfeit, you puppet you!" without seeing him change before my eyes. His spine stiffens, his eyes widen, and his fingers point menacingly.

Having used Shakespeare's words to engage the students emotionally and physically, one can then return to the text for a more reflective discussion of what the words mean to us personally. I always make sure to leave at least a few class periods open for discussion of the text, line by line, to ensure that students understand intellectually what they feel viscerally. The advantage to a performance-based teaching of Shakespeare is that by engaging students vocally, emotionally, and physically, it is then much easier to engage them intellectually because they are invested in the words, the characters, and the story. We always start on our feet, and later we sit and talk.

SIX ELEMENTS OF DRAMA: PLOT, CHARACTER, THEME, DICTION, MUSIC, AND SPECTACLE

Over two thousand years ago, Aristotle's *Poetics* outlined six elements of drama, in order of importance: Plot, Character, Theme, Diction, Music, and Spectacle. Because Shakespeare was foremost a playwright, it is helpful to take a brief look at these six elements as they relate to directing a Shakespeare play in the classroom.

PLOT (ACTION)

To Aristotle, plot was the most important element. One of the purposes of *The 30-Minute Shakespeare* is to provide a script that tells Shakespeare's stories, as opposed to concentrating on one scene. In a thirty-minute edit of a Shakespeare play, some plot elements are necessarily omitted. For the sake of a full understanding of the characters' relationships and motivations, it is helpful to make short plot summaries of each scene so that students are aware of their characters' arcs throughout the play. The scene descriptions in the Folger editions are sufficient to fill in the plot holes. Students can read the descriptions aloud during class time to ensure that the story is clear and that no plot elements are neglected. Additionally, there are one-page charts in the Folger editions of *Shakespeare Set Free*, indicating characters' relations graphically, with lines connecting families and factions to give students a visual representation of what can often be complex interrelationships, particularly in Shakespeare's history plays.

Young actors love action. That is why *The 30-Minute Shakespeare* includes dynamic blocking (stage direction) that allows students to tell the story in a physically dramatic fashion. Characters' movements on the stage are always motivated by the text itself.

CHARACTER

I consider myself a facilitator and a director more than an acting teacher. I want the students' understanding of their characters to spring from the text and the story. From there, I encourage them to consider how their character might talk, walk, stand, sit, eat, and drink. I also urge students to consider characters' motivations, objectives, and relationships, and I will ask pointed questions to that end during the rehearsal process. I try not to show the students how I would perform a scene, but if no ideas are forthcoming from anybody in the class, I will suggest a minimum of two possibilities for how the character might respond.

At times students may want more guidance and examples. Over thirteen years of directing plays in the classroom, I have wavered between wanting all the ideas to come from the students, and deciding that I need to be more of a "director," telling them what I would like to see them doing. It is a fine line, but in recent years I have decided that if I don't see enough dynamic action or characterization, I will step in and "direct" more. But I always make sure to leave room for students to bring themselves into the characters because their own ideas are invariably the best.

THEME (THOUGHTS, IDEAS)

In a typical English classroom, theme will be a big topic for discussion of a Shakespeare play. Using a performance-based method of teaching Shakespeare, an understanding of the play's themes develops from "mining the text" and exploring Shakespeare's words and his story. If the students understand what they are saying and how that relates to their characters and the overall story, the plays' themes will emerge clearly. We always return to the text itself. There are a number of elegant computer programs, such as www.wordle.net, that will count the number of recurring words in a passage and illustrate them graphically. For example, if the word "jealousy" comes up more than any other word in *Othello,* it will appear in a larger font. Seeing the words displayed by size in this way can offer up illuminating insights into the interaction between words in the text and the play's themes. Your computer-minded students might enjoy searching for such tidbits. There are more internet tools and websites in the Additional Resources section at the back of this book.

I cannot overstress the importance of acting out the play in understanding its themes. By embodying the roles of Othello and Iago and reciting their words, students do not simply comprehend the themes intellectually, but understand them kinesthetically, physically, and emotionally. They are essentially *living* the characters' jealousy, pride, and feelings about race. The themes of appearance vs.

reality, good vs. evil, honesty, misrepresentation, and self-knowledge (or lack thereof) become physically felt as well as intellectually understood. Performing Shakespeare delivers a richer understanding than that which comes from just reading the play. Students can now relate the characters' conflicts to their own struggles.

DICTION (LANGUAGE)

If I had to cite one thing I would like my actors to take from their experience of performing a play by William Shakespeare, it is an appreciation and understanding of the beauty of Shakespeare's language. The language is where it all begins and ends. Shakespeare's stories are dramatic, his characters are rich and complex, and his settings are exotic and fascinating, but it is through his language that these all achieve their richness. This leads me to spend more time on language than on any other element of the performance.

Starting with daily vocal warm-ups, many of them using parts of the script or other Shakespearean passages, I consistently emphasize the importance of the words. Young actors often lack experience in speaking clearly and projecting their voices outward, so in addition to comprehension, I emphasize projection, diction, breathing, pacing, dynamics, coloring of words, and vocal energy. *Theatre Games for Young Performers* contains many effective vocal exercises, as does the Folger's *Shakespeare Set Free* series. Consistent emphasis on all aspects of Shakespeare's language, especially on how to speak it effectively, is the most important element to any Shakespeare performance with a young cast.

MUSIC

A little music can go a long way in setting a mood for a thirty-minute Shakespeare play. I usually open the show with a short passage of music to set the tone. Thirty seconds of music played on a boom box operated by a student can provide a nice introduction to the play, create an atmosphere for the audience, and give the actors a sense of place and feeling.

iTunes is a good starting point for choosing your music. Typing in "Shakespeare" or "Hamlet" or "jealousy" (if you are going for a theme) will result in an excellent selection of aural performance enhancers at the very reasonable price of ninety-nine cents each (or free of charge, see Additional Resources section). Likewise, fight sounds, foreboding sounds, weather sounds (rain, thunder), trumpet sounds, etc. are all readily available online at affordable cost. I typically include three sound cues in a play, just enough to enhance but not overpower a production. The boom box operator sits on the far right or left of the stage, not backstage, so he can see the action. This also has the added benefit of having somebody out there with a script, capable of prompting in a pinch.

SPECTACLE

Aristotle considered spectacle the least important aspect of drama. Students tend to be surprised at this since we are used to being bombarded with production values on TV and video, often at the expense of substance. In my early days of putting on student productions, I would find myself hamstrung by my own ambitions in the realm of scenic design.

A simple bench or two chairs set on the stage are sufficient. The sense of "place" can be achieved through language and acting. Simple set dressing, a few key props, and some tasteful, emblematic costume pieces will go a long way toward providing all the "spectacle" you need.

In the stage directions to the plays in *The 30-Minute Shakespeare* series, I make frequent use of two large pillars stage left and right at the Folger Shakespeare Library's Elizabethan Theatre. I also have characters frequently entering and exiting from "stage rear." Your stage will have a different layout. Take a good look at the performing space you will be using and see if there are any elements that can be incorporated into your own stage directions. Is there a balcony? Can characters enter from the audience? (Make sure that they can get there from backstage, unless you want them waiting in the lobby until their entrance, which may be impractical.) If possible, make sure to rehearse in that space a few times to fix any technical issues and perhaps discover a few fun staging variations that will add pizzazz and dynamics to your own show.

The real spectacle is in the telling of the tale. Wooden swords are handy for characters that need them. Students should be warned at the outset that playing with swords outside of the scene is verboten. Letters, moneybags, and handkerchiefs should all have plentiful duplicates kept in a small prop box, as well as with a stage manager, because they tend to disappear in the hands of adolescents. After every rehearsal and performance, I recommend you personally sweep the rehearsal or performance area immediately for stray props. It is amazing what gets left behind.

Ultimately, the performances are about language and human drama, not set pieces, props, and special effects. Fake blood, glitter, glass, and liquids have no place on the stage; they are a recipe for disaster, or, at the very least, a big mess. On the other hand, the props that are employed can often be used effectively to convey character, as in Bardolph's aforementioned relationship with his wineskin.

PITFALLS AND SOLUTIONS

Putting on a play in a high school classroom is not easy. There are problems with enthusiasm, attitude, attention, and line memorization, to name a few. As anybody who has directed a play will tell you, it is always darkest before the dawn. My experience is that after one or two days of utter despair just before the play goes up, show day breaks and the play miraculously shines. To quote a recurring gag in one of my favorite movies, *Shakespeare in Love*: "It's a mystery."

ENTHUSIASM, FRUSTRATION, AND DISCIPLINE

Bring the enthusiasm yourself. Feed on the energy of the eager students, and others will pick up on that. Keep focused on the task at hand. Arrive prepared. Enthusiasm comes as you make headway. Ultimately, it helps to remind the students that a play is fun. I try to focus on the positive attributes of the students, rather than the ones that drive me crazy. This is easier said than done, but it is important. One season, I yelled at the group two days in a row. On day two of yelling, they tuned me out, and it took me a while to win them back. I learned my lesson; since then I've tried not to raise my voice out of anger or frustration. As I grow older and more mature, it is important for me to lead by example. It has been years since I yelled at a student group. If I am disappointed in their work or their behavior, I will express my disenchantment in words, speaking from the heart as somebody who cares about them and cares about our performance and our experience together. I find that fundamentally, young people want to please, to do well, and to be liked. If there is a serious discipline problem, I will hand it over to the regular classroom teacher, the administrator, or the parent.

LINE MEMORIZATION

Students may have a hard time memorizing lines. In these cases, see if you can pair them up with a "buddy" and existing friend who will run lines with them in person or over the phone after school. If students do not have such a "buddy," I volunteer to run lines with them myself. If serious line memorization problems arise that cannot be solved through work, then two students can switch parts if it is early enough in the rehearsal process. For doubled roles, the scene with fewer lines can go to the actor who is having memorization problems. Additionally, a few passages or lines can be cut. Again, it is important to address these issues early. Later cuts become more problematic as other actors have already memorized their cues. I have had to do late cuts about twice in thirteen years. While they have gotten us out of jams, it is best to assess early whether a student will have line memorization problems, and deal with the problem sooner rather than later.

In production, always keep several copies of the script backstage, as well as cheat sheets indicating cues, entrances, and scene changes. Make a prop list, indicating props for each scene, as well as props that are the responsibility of individual actors. Direct the Stage Manager and an Assistant Stage Manager to keep track of these items, and on show days, personally double-check if you can.

In thirteen years of preparing an inner-city public high school English class for a public performance on a field trip to the Folger Secondary School Shakespeare Festival, my groups and I have been beset by illness, emotional turmoil, discipline problems, stage fright, adolescent angst, midlife crises (not theirs), and all manner of other emergencies, including acts of God and nature. Despite the difficulties and challenges inherent in putting on a Shakespeare play with a group of young people, one amazing fact stands out in my experience. Here is how many times a student has been absent for show day: Zero. Somehow, everybody has always made it to the show, and the show has gone on. How can this be? It's a mystery.

✳ PERFORMANCE NOTES: *AS YOU LIKE IT*

I directed this version of *As You Like It* with a group of ninth graders in 1999. The play is ideal for young actors, as it allows them to enter a romantic new world full of colorful characters and beguiling language.

These notes are the result of my own review of the performance video. They are not intended to be the "definitive" performance notes for all productions of *As You Like It*. Your production will be unique to you and your cast. That is the magic of live theater. What is interesting about these notes is that many of the performance details I mention were not part of the original stage directions. They either emerged spontaneously on performance day or were developed by students in rehearsal after the stage directions had been written into the script.

Some of these pieces of stage business work like a charm. Others fall flat. Still others are unintentionally hilarious. My favorites are the ones that arise directly from the students themselves and demonstrate a union between actor and character, as if that individual has become a vehicle for the character he is playing. To witness a fifteen-year-old young woman "become" Rosalind as Shakespeare's words leave her mouth is a memorable moment indeed.

SCENE 1 (ACT I, SCENE III)

As the first scene begins, courtly music imparts a sense of place. These thirty-minute stagings do not require elaborate set pieces, and music (played on a boom box in this production) can set the tone quite well. If a cast member can play a classical instrumental snippet live, then so much the better. I am continually impressed with the power of music to set a mood, particularly at the top of a play.

As the narrator introduces the scene, Duke Frederick and Duke Senior enter. Duke Frederick points to Duke Senior, banishing him, and Duke Senior exits. We use simple staging to introduce the characters and illustrate a major plot point. This theatrical device underscores my belief that in order for audiences to "get" Shakespeare, they must first "get" the story. This version of *As You Like It* uses music and tableaux at the outset to bring viewers into the world of the play.

The Duke's banishment of Rosalind is swift, unexpected, and terrifying, since it comes with a death threat. Rosalind and Celia must react physically to the news. Their bodies and faces should depict fear and confusion. Young actors often hold back on their responses, not wishing to embarrass themselves. If Rosalind is encouraged to fall to her knees at the Duke's side, the power of this staging may elicit a more emotional verbal response from the actor as well. When the body illustrates an extreme emotion it is sometimes easier for the voice and facial expressions to follow suit. Thus, careful blocking is a good tool for illustrating plot and character as well as eliciting emotion from performers.

We achieve an effective stage picture by placing Rosalind on her knees, head bowed into hands. Celia kneels over her with her hand on Rosalind's back, and the Duke stands upstage with his back fully to the audience. (Full rear blocking such as the Duke's is of course best employed when an actor is not speaking. Words are easily lost when not spoken out toward the audience.) Tableaux are an effective rehearsal tool, useful for exploring simple visual statements that illustrate the text, clarify plot points, and illuminate relationships.

In this production of *As You Like It*, the young actor playing Duke Senior had a strong physical presence and a powerful voice. When he said to Celia, "You are a fool," he was almost shouting, and he had a knack for emphasizing certain words to achieve maximum effect: "You *die*." Actors should be encouraged to experiment with which words (or syllables) to stress in a speech, since changes in emphasis can elicit varying meanings. This shows players that *how* the words are spoken greatly affects their meaning and interpretation.

Simple costume and prop choices help actors color their roles. Duke Senior had a cape that he threw over his shoulder dramatically before striding off stage. As Celia announced that she would call herself "Aliena," she pulled a fan from her cape and fanned herself coyly. This added a touch of comic whimsy to her character.

When Rosalind suggested that Touchstone travel with her and Celia responded, "Hell go along o'er the wide world with me," she skipped and danced in a circle about the stage before exiting. This action physically described Touchstone's spirit, while also giving us more insight into Celia's merry humor.

SCENE 2 (ACT II, SCENE I)

As we transition from the Court into the forest, prerecorded bird whistles provide a nice acoustic scene setting. There are two stools wrapped in brown wrapping paper to look like stumps, and a few leaves and stones scattered about the stage complete the set dressing. There is something satisfying about a minimalist approach to scenic design. It allows actors and audience to fill in the picture with Shakespeare's words and their imagination. My experience has been shaped by fourteen years of participation in a student festival; eight schools a day tread the boards at the Folger Library, leaving little time for elaborate scenery.

If your situation differs, and you have the resources and inclination to spend more time on scenic design, this too can be satisfying, especially if there are members of your group who can contribute creatively. I prefer a scaled-down approach, but I acknowledge my own tastes and the uniqueness of my venue. I encourage you to explore every aspect of the spectacle that will enhance your theatrical experience. I do urge directors to continually return to Shakespeare's rich text as their primary dramatic source.

On the line "sermons in stones," Duke Senior picks up a stone, puts it to his ear like a seashell, and passes it on to the other group members, who likewise raise it to their ears to listen. The final actor shrugs and places the stone back down on the stage. When Jaques enters, he gives Senior a special forest handshake (of the actor's invention). On Jaques's famous "Seven Ages of Man" speech, he puts his hand on each of his three seated comrades' shoulders during each of his final three phrases: "Sans teeth (first comrade), sans eyes (second comrade), sans taste (third comrade), sans everything (Jaques alone)." These characters are "brothers in exile" so it is nice to have some group sequences to illustrate their unity.

This staging serves to reiterate the inclusive nature of the speech. This journey from birth to death is one we all share. After "sans everything" all four men bow their heads in silence, which gets a laugh.

The fine line between comedy and tragedy fascinates me. That unison head bowing could just as easily have resulted in a thoughtful moment of silence from the audience as they absorbed the fact of our own mortality, but this adolescent audience chose laughter as a response. The key is for the actors to play it straight. Perhaps the sincerity of their somber physical response to Jaques's speech was what tickled the audience's funny bone. Regarding the timing of the speech, it is important to *pause* after "sans everything." It is during that pause that the players solemnly digest Jaques's weighty words, and where the laughter has a chance to emerge. When blocking this scene I did not predict audience laughter, but I was happy it occurred. There are other moments (such as Juliet's death) that do not invite laughter, and if it occurs, we must study the cause to prevent it in the future. Likewise, when audiences grace us with their laughter, we should try to replicate the circumstances. It is not an exact science but it is worthy of study! Make sure to have at least one rehearsal in front of an audience to gauge potential responses.

When Orlando enters and encounters the exiled lords, his fear and bravado stand in contrast to the mellowness of the peacefully snacking forest-dwellers. This is a funny moment because the contrast between Orlando and the foresters is evident in their body language. Whereas Orlando spins about suspiciously and brandishes his sword, the forest men gnaw languidly on their food and pay him no mind.

This scene in our 1993 performance ends on a rousing note, with the band of foresters clapping out a rhythm and Jaques lagging behind the rest, busting out a few unique and personal dance moves. Personality cannot be taught, but providing a rehearsal environment of experimentation and fun can encourage its expression. After each verse, the entire group shouts out a loud "Heigh Ho!" and they exit the stage with a loud and simultaneous cry of "This life is most jolly!"

SCENE 3 (ACT III, SCENE II)

This version of *As You Like It* will always stand out in my memory because it featured award-winning sheep. There are no small parts: three young actors played the part of sheep by getting down on all fours covered in white wool blankets, wearing little leather sheep ears. The three sheep gave Touchstone great focus as he spoke. They seemed to react to his words as if they understood English. These fine animals gave attention to another actor on stage while retaining their individual qualities, and they exhibited group unity by moving together and not stepping on each other's "baahs"! The Folgers Festival commentators gave the sheep (who doubled as goats later in the play) an award for "commitment to character" and they received big laughs whenever they appeared. In subsequent years directing students, I have used these stellar sheep as an example of how to do great work with a small role—and have fun with it!

In this scene, Corin and Touchstone engage in a battle of the wits over the merits of country versus city living. The two actors end up in each other's faces physically, nose to nose, adding a nice menacing edge to otherwise cordial banter. Acquiescing to Touchstone's superior wit, Corin pats him on the shoulder on the line, "You have too courtly a wit for me; I'll rest."

The blocking of this interchange might have been more successful if Corin had actually put his arm around Touchstone. The physical voyage from nose-to-nose to arm-in-arm would have been more satisfying than a pat on the shoulder. It helps to experiment with varying levels of physical commitment in a scene. In this case I took the "safe" route, or the path of least resistance. Next time I will encourage the actors to explore a deeper level of physical commitment to the relationship. If arm-in-arm does not work, one can always revert to the former blocking. The point is to take the physicalization in rehearsal as far as you need to yield satisfying results.

As Rosalind enters reciting poetry, Touchstone responds by twirling about her gracefully, ultimately procuring a rose from his cape, kneeling, and presenting it to her, resulting in a big "aww" from the adolescent audience. Throughout the play, the actor playing Touchstone used his natural physical grace to imbue his character with charm. If an actor has skills or training in dance or other disciplines, try to incorporate them into the play. The best ideas and pieces of stage business often come directly from the actors and their unique talents.

When Rosalind and Orlando meet in this scene, they stand inappropriately close to one another, delighting Rosalind and confusing Orlando, who is attracted to this character while believing she is a man. As with other aspects of speech and movement, physical distance between characters on stage speaks volumes about their relationship. Whereas Corin and Touchstone's nose-to-nose stance indicates combativeness, Rosalind and Orlando's proximity suggests intimacy.

Look for staging patterns that can be repeated to give rhythms to a production, like motifs in a piece of music. By combining Shakespeare's great language with our actors' minds, bodies, and spirits, we create together a living, breathing work of art on stage.

We had a long pause with a bare stage between Scenes 3 and 4. I had all the narrators wear capes to signify their roles, but this required actors to find their capes quickly between scenes, which did not happen. As with elaborate scene changes, which needlessly slow the story's momentum, unnecessary costuming conceits impede the dramatic flow. In subsequent years I streamlined these scene changes, with excellent results.

SCENE 4 (ACT III, SCENE III)

As if the long and bungled scene change were not enough, the narrator in Scene 4 completely forgot her first line. She stood on stage frozen in horror until I retrieved my script from under my seat and prompted her from the audience, a technique I made sure to prepare for in future years. When working with adolescent actors, one must always have a Plan B!

The goats made another appearance during Touchstone and Audrey's entrance and generated a nice response from the audience. The sheep (or goats) got a bigger laugh each time they appeared, so I decided to employ the rule of three and add one more "baa" to the narrator's line in the following scene. (The student playing the narrator had just been onstage as a goat.) There is a rule of three in comedy. Use it. It works.

Touchstone's cape had bells on it, which the actor used to his advantage by walking and prancing to the rhythm of their jingling. I encourage players to use simple but fun props and costume pieces as character helpers because our clothes tells a lot about who we are. Touchstone's red and black velour cape seemed to imbue him with the superpowers of the fool! But the true power came from this ninth grader's sense of playfulness and joy and his love of language and whimsy. When combined with Shakespeare's unforgettable words and stories it proved a potent pairing.

Audrey and Touchstone walk off arm in arm at scene's end, followed by bleating goats that shove and jostle for position, providing a hilarious animal counterpoint to the human drama. Remember, there are no small roles.

SCENE 5 (ACT III, SCENE V)

This scene begins auspiciously with the narrator still wearing his goat ears from the previous scene and inserting a well timed "baa" after the phrase "Nothing is simple in love." Silvius enters running and sliding, stopping at Phebe's ankles, which he hugs with amorous abandon. A tug of war follows, with Rosalind trying to hold off a grasping Phebe and Phebe trying to fend off a clutching Silvius. The characters lose their grip, and Phebe falls to the floor, spread-eagled. Young actors usually have a lot of fun with these physical sequences.

The actress playing Rosalind enjoyed her character and spoke her lines with conviction and power. The young actor portraying Silvius had no problem sliding on the ground on his knees and letting himself be dragged all over the stage by Phebe. I have no magic formula for eliciting such commitment from actors, except by demonstrating my own devotion to the life of the play and trying to create an environment where young actors feel safe. When they have enough confidence, they will throw themselves fully into their roles.

SCENE 6 (ACT V, SCENE II)

There is some enjoyable tag-team dialogue in this scene as each of the lovers in turn proclaim their love for their intended, with each sequence ending with Rosalind's "and I for no woman." Because the loose ends of the plot are coming together at this point, Rosalind must be very clear *whom* she is addressing in each sequence by looking each player directly in the eye. Actors must always remember that they know the play better than their audience does. Our job is to bring them into the world of the story. Vocal diction and projection, coupled with clear physicalizations, will go far in helping the audience understand the plot.

SCENE 7 (ACT V, SCENE IV)

Magical wedding music at the top of the scene sets the tone for a merry entrance and a comedic ending. The ladies enter with flowers, all facing front. Hymen snaps her fingers and all freeze, which provides good focus on Hymen for her speech. Just for fun, try having two of the previously frozen actors startle each other when their eyes meet.

The final song recited by the cast in unison brings the play to a rousing, unified, and lively close. Because the entire cast is gathering onstage, audiences may think the play has ended and begin their applause prematurely. Assign one actor to begin the song as the rest of the cast enters so that by the time everyone is on stage, all are reciting/singing the song. This will delay the audience's applause until the true end of the play.

Thus ends our merry tale, as the group claps, sings, and steps in unison. A springtime feeling washes over the world when we magically join a group of ninth graders with the poetic words of William Shakespeare.

Live theater is magical. It is the most dynamic form of entertainment available to us. There is nothing like the interchange between actors and audience, that vibrant energy that is created in the theater. *As You Like It* is one of Shakespeare's most beloved comedies, and we are fortunate to be able to continue bringing it to life, especially with young performers who can give it the vitality it deserves.

✳ *AS YOU LIKE IT:*
SET AND PROP LIST

SET PIECES:

Table

Two chairs

Tall stool with burlap or paper covering to look like short tree

Short stool with burlap or paper covering to look like tree stump

Throne

PROPS:

SCENE 1:

Teacups

Vase

Candleholder with candle

Flowers

Fan for Celia

SCENE 2:

Leaves

Rock for Duke Senior

Packs for forest dwellers

Bread and fruit to put in packs

Sword for Orlando

SCENE 3:

Orlando's love notes

Crook for Corin

Rose for Touchstone

SCENE 4:

Bucket for Audrey

Two handkerchiefs for Touchstone

SCENE 5:

Handkerchief for Narrator

BENJAMIN BANNEKER SENIOR HIGH SCHOOL *presents*

As You Like It

By William Shakespeare

Folger Shakespeare Library Secondary School Festival

Tuesday, March 11th 1999

Instructor: Mr. David Ritzer | Guest Director: Mr. Nick Newlin

CAST:

Act 1, Scene 3.
A room in Duke Frederick's palace
NARRATOR: Dennis Harris, Jr.

CELIA, *Rosalind's cousin, daughter to Duke Frederick:* Jennifer Butler

ROSALIND, *daughter to Duke Senior:* Lauren Thompson

DUKE FREDERICK, *the usurping duke:* D'Angelo Gore

Act 2, Scene 1. The forest of Arden
NARRATOR: Leisha Walker

DUKE SENIOR, *the exiled duke, brother to Duke Frederick:* John Clarke

Lords attending Duke Senior in exile:

AMIENS: Dennis Harris Jr.

JAQUES: Daniel Philip

"LORD T": Toussaint Tingling-Clemmons

ORLANDO: *Youngest son of Sir Rowland de Bois:* Jon-Claude Simms

Act 3, Scene 2. The forest of Arden
NARRATOR Chanel Sarantis

CORIN, *a shepherd:* Marcus Richarson

TOUCHSTONE, *a court Fool:* Marcus Watson

ROSALIND: Savannah Briscoe

CELIA: Leisha Walker

ORLANDO: Jon-Claude Simms

SHEEP: Dennis Harris Jr., John Clarke, D'Angelo Gore

Act 3, Scene 3. The forest of Arden
NARRATOR: Leisha Walker

TOUCHSTONE: Marcus Watson

AUDREY, *a goat-keeper:* Castina J. Watson

GOATS: Dennis Harris Jr., John Clarke, D'Angelo Gore

Act 3, Scene 5. The forest of Arden
NARRATOR: Dennis Harris Jr.

SILVIUS: *a young shepherd in love:* Toussaint Tingling-Clemmons

PHEBE: *a disdainful shepherdess:* Bintou Kouyate

CELIA: Leisha Walker

ROSALIND: Alexandra Lockamy

Act 5, Scene 2. The forest of Arden
NARRATOR: Leisha Walker

ORLANDO: Jon-Claude Simms

OLIVER *Orlando's older brother:* Dennis Harris Jr.

ROSALIND: Eva James

PHEBE: Lauren Taylor

SILVIUS: Toussaint Tingling-Clemmons

Act 5, Scene 4. The forest of Arden
NARRATOR: D'Angelo Gore.

DUKE SENIOR: John Clarke.

ORLANDO: Jon-Claude Simms

ROSALIND: Lauren Thompson

OLIVER: Dennis Harris Jr.

CELIA: Jennifer Butler

SILVIUS: Toussaint Tingling-Clemmons.

PHEBE: Chanel Sarantis

TOUCHSTONE: Marcus Watson

AUDREY: Castina J. Watson

HYMEN, *Goddess of Marriage:* Kneiss Johnson

Stage Crew:
STAGE MANAGER: Malachi Cunningham

SETS: Durriyyah Johnson

COSTUMES: Siu-Lin Robinson, Shika Duncan, Castina J. Watson

PROPS: Deonna Ball

MUSIC: Alvin Hough Jr.

PROGRAMS: Dottye Gay

ADDITIONAL RESOURCES

SHAKESPEARE

Shakespeare Set Free: Teaching Romeo and Juliet, Macbeth and a Midsummer Night's Dream
Peggy O'Brien, Ed., Teaching Shakespeare Institute
Washington Square Press
New York, 1993

Shakespeare Set Free: Teaching Hamlet and Henry IV, Part 1
Peggy O'Brien, Ed., Teaching Shakespeare Institute
Washington Square Press
New York, 1994

Shakespeare Set Free: Teaching Twelfth Night and Othello
Peggy O'Brien, Ed., Teaching Shakespeare Institute
Washington Square Press
New York, 1995

The *Shakespeare Set Free* series is an invaluable resource with lesson plans, activites, handouts, and excellent suggestions for rehearsing and performing Shakespeare plays in a classroom setting.

ShakesFear and How to Cure It!
Ralph Alan Cohen
Prestwick House, Inc.
Delaware, 2006

The Friendly Shakespeare: A Thoroughly Painless Guide to the Best of the Bard
Norrie Epstein
Penguin Books
New York, 1994

Brush Up Your Shakespeare!
Michael Macrone
Cader Books
New York, 1990

Shakespeare's Insults: Educating Your Wit
Wayne F. Hill and Cynthia J. Ottchen
Three Rivers Press
New York, 1991

Practical Approaches to Teaching Shakespeare
Peter Reynolds
Oxford University Press
New York, 1991

Scenes From Shakespeare:
A Workbook for Actors
Robin J. Holt
McFarland and Co.
London, 1988

101 Theatre Games for Drama
Teachers, Classroom Teachers
& Directors
Mila Johansen
Players Press Inc.
California, 1994

THEATER AND PERFORMANCE

Impro: Improvisation and the Theatre
Keith Johnstone
Routledge Books
London, 1982

A Dictionary of Theatre Anthropology:
The Secret Art of the Performer
Eugenio Barba and Nicola Savarese
Routledge
London, 1991

THEATER GAMES

Theatre Games for Young Performers
Maria C. Novelly
Meriwether Publishing
Colorado, 1990

Improvisation for the Theater
Viola Spolin
Northwestern University Press
Illinois, 1983

Theater Games for Rehearsal:
A Director's Handbook
Viola Spolin
Northwestern University Press
Illinois, 1985

PLAY DIRECTING

Theater and the Adolescent Actor:
Building a Successful School Program
Camille L. Poisson
Archon Books
Connecticut, 1994

Directing for the Theatre
W. David Sievers
Wm. C. Brown, Co.
Iowa, 1965

The Director's Vision: Play Direction
from Analysis to Production
Louis E. Catron
Mayfield Publishing Co.
California, 1989

INTERNET RESOURCES

http://www.folger.edu
The Folger Shakespeare Library's
website has lesson plans, primary
sources, study guides, images,
workshops, programs for teachers
and students, and much more. The
definitive Shakespeare website for
educators, historians and all lovers
of the Bard.

http://www.shakespeare.mit.edu.
The Complete Works of
William Shakespeare.
All complete scripts for *The
30-Minute Shakespeare* series were
originally downloaded from this site
before editing. Links to other internet
resources.

http://www.LoMonico.com/
Shakespeare-and-Media.htm
http://shakespeare-and-media
.wikispaces.com
Michael LoMonico is Senior
Consultant on National Education
for the Folger Shakespeare Library.
His *Seminar Shakespeare 2.0* offers a
wealth of information on how to use
exciting new approaches and online
resources for teaching Shakespeare.

http://www.freesound.org.
A collaborative database of sounds
and sound effects.

http://www.wordle.net.
A program for creating "word clouds"
from the text that you provide. The
clouds give greater prominence to
words that appear more frequently in
the source text.

http://www.opensourceshakespeare
.org.
This site has good searching capacity.

http://shakespeare.palomar.edu/
default.htm
Excellent links and searches

http://shakespeare.com/
Write like Shakespeare,
Poetry Machine, tag cloud

http://www.shakespeare-online.com/

http://www.bardweb.net/

http://www.rhymezone.com/
shakespeare/
Good searchable word and phrase
finder.
Or by lines:
http://www.rhymezone.com/
shakespeare/toplines/

http://shakespeare.mcgill.ca/
Shakespeare and Performance
research team

http://www.enotes.com/william-
shakespeare

Needless to say, the internet goes on and on with valuable Shakespeare resources.
The ones listed here are excellent starting points and will set you on your way in the
great adventure that is Shakespeare.

NICK NEWLIN has performed a comedy and variety act for international audiences for twenty-seven years. Since 1996, he has conducted an annual play directing residency affiliated with the Folger Shakespeare Library in Washington, D.C. Newlin received a BA with Honors from Harvard University in 1982 and an MA in Theater with an emphasis in Play Directing from the University of Maryland in 1996.

THE 30-MINUTE SHAKESPEARE

AS YOU LIKE IT
978-1-935550-06-8

THE COMEDY OF ERRORS
978-1-935550-08-2

HAMLET
978-1-935550-24-2

HENRY IV, PART 1
978-1-935550-11-2

HENRY V
978-1-935550-38-9

JULIUS CAESAR
978-1-935550-29-7

KING LEAR
978-1-935550-09-9

LOVE'S LABOR'S LOST
978-1-935550-07-5

MACBETH
978-1-935550-02-0

A MIDSUMMER NIGHT'S DREAM
978-1-935550-00-6

THE MERCHANT OF VENICE
978-1-935550-32-7

THE MERRY WIVES OF WINDSOR
978-1-935550-05-1

MUCH ADO ABOUT NOTHING
978-1-935550-03-7

OTHELLO
978-1-935550-10-5

RICHARD III
978-1-935550-39-6

ROMEO AND JULIET
978-1-935550-01-3

THE TAMING OF THE SHREW
978-1-935550-33-4

THE TEMPEST
978-1-935550-28-0

TWELFTH NIGHT
978-1-935550-04-4

THE TWO GENTLEMEN OF VERONA
978-1-935550-25-9

THE 30-MINUTE SHAKESPEARE ANTHOLOGY
978-1-935550-33-4

All plays $9.95, available in print and eBook editions in bookstores everywhere

"A truly fun, emotional, and sometimes magical first experience . . . guided by a sagacious, knowledgeable, and intuitive educator." —Library Journal

PHOTOCOPYING AND PERFORMANCE RIGHTS

There is no royalty for performing any series of *The 30-Minute Shakespeare* in a classroom or on a stage. The publisher hereby grants unlimited photocopy permission for one series of performances to all acting groups that have purchased the play. If a group stages a performance, please post a comment and/or photo to our Facebook page; we'd love to hear about it!

CPSIA information can be obtained
at www.ICGtesting.com
Printed in the USA
JSHW041952230523
42123JS00009B/599